Cycling

SPORTS
SKILLS

Paul Mason

W

FRANKLIN WATTS

Franklin Watts
First published in Great Britain in 2015 by The Watts Publishing Group

Copyright © The Watts Publishing Group 2015

Credits
Series Editor: Adrian Cole
Art direction: Peter Scoulding
Series designed and created for
 Franklin Watts by Storeybooks
Designer: Rita Storey
Editor: Nicola Barber
Photography: Tudor Photography,
Banbury (unless otherwise stated)

Dewey number 796.6
HB ISBN 978 1 4451 4134 3
Library ebook ISBN 978 1 4451 4343 9

Printed in China

Franklin Watts
An imprint of Hachette Children's Group
Part of The Watts Publishing Group
Carmelite House
50 Victoria Embankment
London EC4Y 0DZ

An Hachette UK Company
www.hachette.co.uk

www.franklinwatts.co.uk

Note: At the time of going to press, the statistics and profiles in this book were up to date. However, due to some cyclists' active participation in the sport, it is possible that some of these may now be out of date.

Picture credits
Shutterstock/Connel p.6; istock p.7 (top), p.9 (top) and p.19 (left); Shutterstock/Radu Razvan p.7 (bottom) and p.8 (top); Shutterstock/karamysh pp.6-7, 9 (bottom); Shutterstock/homydesign p.8 (bottom) and p.18; Shutterstock/donatas1205 p.9 (middle); Shutterstock/Pitsanu Kraichana p.11 (top); Shutterstock/Andy.M p.11 (bottom); Shutterstock/ecadphoto p.12 (bottom); Shutterstock/Andy Lidstone p.14; Shutterstock/domaniczky p.19 (right); Corbis/Troy Wayrynen/NewSport p21 (top); Shutterstock/Featureflash p.25 (top); Shutterstock/Rena Schild p.26; Paul Mason p.27.

Cover images: Tudor Photography, Banbury.

All photos posed by models. Thanks to Matt Gittings, Emma Pitt, Sam Serruya and Cameron Swarbrick.

The Publisher would like to thank Adrian Pitt and the Palmer Park Velo Cycling Club for all their help.

Previously published by Franklin Watts as Know Your Sport Cycling.

Taking part in sport is a fun way to get fit, but like any form of physical exercise it has an element of risk, particularly if you are unfit, overweight or suffer from any medical conditions. It is advisable to consult a healthcare professional before beginning any programme of exercise.

Contents

What is Cycling?

"Now that," said the famous adventurer and writer Jack London, "is something that makes life worth living!" He was talking about cycling, one of the world's most popular kinds of exercise.

Cycling as Transport

Cycling is not only good exercise, it is also an important form of transport for millions of people around the world. In many cities, a bike is by far the fastest way to get around. Cyclists can often use special cycle lanes to whizz past lines of cars sitting in traffic jams.

A bike is a much less expensive way of getting around than a car. And unlike motorised transport, bikes do not pump harmful pollution into the air every time they are used.

Cycling is fantastic exercise that helps to keep you fit and healthy. It's also a great way of getting from place to place.

It's a Fact

In 1884, Thomas Stevens rode a penny-farthing (see page 7) from the west to the east coast of the USA. Then, between 1885 and 1886, he carried on from London, through Europe, the Middle East, China and Japan, to become the first cyclist to ride around the world.

6

Bike Racing

Ever since bicycles were invented, people have been racing on them. But bike racing first became famous around the world in 1903. That year the toughest bike race on Earth, the Tour de France, was first run. The Tour lasted 19 days, and covered up to 400 kilometres in a day. The racers often had to carry on riding into the night to finish each day's distance.

Today, the Tour is still the most famous of road races, but there are many other kinds of bike racing, too. Cross-country, BMX, downhill and endurance racing are all increasingly popular.

The First Bicycles

Early bikes had solid 'tyres', which made them very uncomfortable! They also had a giant front wheel and a tiny rear wheel. They were called 'penny-farthings', after large (penny) and small (farthing) coins of the time. Then, in the late 1800s, bikes more like today's began to appear. The wheels were the same size, and the bikes had air-filled tyres. These new bikes were much easier and more comfortable to ride, and by 1900 a craze for cycling had spread around the world. Now, everyone can join in the fun.

The péloton (main group of riders) of the Tour de France – the world's most famous bike race – rides on a wet, slippery road in Saint-Remy-de-Provence in July 2014. The Tour often visits other countries, but most of the racing takes place in France.

The Best Bike for You

It's important to get the right kind and size of bike, whether you use it for racing, travelling around or to keep fit – otherwise you will not enjoy riding it. The bike you choose then needs to be set up so that it's comfortable and transfers your pedalling effort into speed.

The Right Kind of Bike

Having the right type of bike makes cycling much more enjoyable. There are many different kinds, including:

- Mountain bikes, which can be ridden anywhere but are relatively slow on the road.
- Road bikes, which have skinny wheels and tyres, and are very light. These are good on the road – and rubbish off it!
- Cyclo-cross bikes, which are basically road bikes with fatter, knobbly tyres. These are almost as quick as road bikes on the road, and can be used for off-road riding too.
- Specialist bikes such as BMX, time trial or track bikes are not designed for general use.

This Tour de France cyclist is riding a time-trial bike that makes use of the latest technology to slice through the air as efficiently as possible. The cyclist must be able to maintain the riding position throughout the race.

A rider competes at the Sangalhos Velodrome in Portugal. Track bikes are very specialised – they have no brakes and one gear, so they are really only suitable for riding on a velodrome or similar track.

Saddle angle
The saddle is usually most comfortable when it is parallel to the ground. Some riders even use a spirit level to make sure it's exactly flat.

The right size frame
When your feet are on the ground, you need a 3–10cm gap between your body and the frame here.

Handlebars
Higher handlebars are usually more comfortable. Lower handlebars are more aerodynamic and allow greater speed. It is best to start with the handlebars about level with the saddle, and make adjustments from there.

Saddle height
When you sit on the saddle with your heel on the pedal at its lowest point, your leg should be nearly straight.

A well set-up bike is comfortable and fun to ride.

Chain

Setting Up Your Bike

It is important to have a good, strong lock for your bike.

Setting up your bike means adjusting the saddle height and handlebars to find the best riding position for you. A well set-up bike travels faster, because it transfers your pedalling power to the back wheel well. Badly set-up bikes can cause injuries to your knees or back.

People adjust their bike set-up to suit the kind of riding they are doing: downhill racers and BMX riders have the saddle height very low, road racers have it set high. The photo guide on this page gives you a good place to start.

Safety Checks

Check your bike regularly to make sure it is safe:

- Do the brakes come on properly?
- Are the handlebars completely secure?
- Is the seat also secure?
- Are the wheels fastened as tightly as possible?

Clothing and Safety

It's possible to cycle wearing almost anything, but a bit of thought about what you put on makes cycling a lot more comfortable. By wearing bright colours and reflective gear you can make it safer too.

Ideal Bike Clothing

The best clothes for cycling are quite tight fitting. Loose clothes are generally a bad idea because once you get up to speed, they flap around and get in the way. This is especially true with trousers: if a trouser leg meets up with a bike chain, disaster can rapidly follow!

A well-equipped young rider.

Helmet protects the rider's head.

Cycling glasses protect the rider's eyes.

Waterproof jacket can be rolled up small and stored in the back pocket of the top.

Stretchy top is warm but doesn't get sweaty.

Gloves cushion the rider's hands.

Stretchy shorts with special padding where they touch the saddle.

Special shoes are pressed into the pedals to clip on to them. Most riders are faster using this type of shoe and pedal.

The Golden Rules

DO
- Ride well clear of the kerb.
- Be positive.
- Make eye contact so that you know drivers have seen you.
- Signal clearly.
- Avoid riding on the inside of large vehicles such as lorries – they may not be able to see you.
- Use your lights when it begins to get dark or in poor visibility.
- Make sure other road users and pedestrians can see you – wear bright-coloured clothing during the day and reflective clothing at night.
- Watch out for car doors opening suddenly.
- Wear a helmet.

DON'T
- Cycle with headphones or use your phone whilst cycling.
- Cycle on the pavement.
- Change direction suddenly without warning.
- Cycle through red lights.
- Cycle up a one-way street the wrong way.

Having a bell means you can warn people you are coming. This is very handy if there are walkers around, since they often forget to check if a bike is coming before stepping into the road to cross it.

No Parking!

The parking problems in big cities could be solved if more people rode their bikes to get to work. Approximately 20 bikes (or 40 Brompton folding bikes) can be parked in the same space as one car.

Fitness and Training

Cycling is a great way of getting fit, because it is easy to work it into your normal daily routine. Instead of being driven to school, you can go on your bike. You might even persuade your mum or dad to come along for the ride!

Fitness Benefits

There are lots of benefits to taking exercise and getting fit:

- It makes your bones, heart, lungs and every muscle in your body stronger.
- Studies show that children who take regular exercise perform better at school.
- Health problems such as back pain, sleeplessness and digestive problems are helped by exercise.

Cycling is especially good because it can be done at any pace.

Even very unfit people can go cycling, starting slowly and building up speed as they get fitter.

Joining a Cycling Club

If you become serious about cycling and aim to take part in competitions, the best way to improve your fitness and technique is to join an official cycling club. A club is also somewhere to meet up with other young cyclists, and try all the different kinds of cycling until you find the one that's best for you.

Cycling clubs aren't just about training – they're usually a good place to make friends, too.

Next time you're going somewhere, ask yourself, "Could I go on my bike instead?" The answer is usually yes: almost any journey under a few kilometres long can be made by bike.

• It's a Fact

James Moore is said to have won the first-ever bike race, in 1868 in France. That same year, he also won the first-ever Paris–Rouen race. Cycling wasn't as well paid then, and Moore had to pay his own train fare home from Rouen. Not only that, his bike was stolen from outside a café near the finish!

Young cyclists working with their coach, who is explaining the training he wants them to do.

Training Together

At a cycling club, the riders train together, pushing each other to higher fitness levels than they could achieve on their own. When you ride as a group, there's always someone who races away from the front, forcing everyone else to sprint to keep up!

Setting off on a training ride together.

Working with a Coach

One of the big pluses of joining a cycling club is that you get to work with a qualified coach. A good coach will be able to give you advice on just about any aspect of cycling, including:

- What kind of competition he or she thinks you are best at (road, track, mountain bike, etc.).
- Your riding style and technique.
- The best way to set up your bike.
- Training and other fitness issues, such as the best foods to eat.

Choosing a Club

It is a good idea to pick the club you join carefully, because not all clubs specialise in every kind of cycling. If you are already interested in mountain biking, for example, check that the club has other mountain-biking members and a mountain-bike coach.

13

Cadence and Gears

'Cadence' means pedalling speed. Pedalling in the right gear and at the right speed are essential cycling skills. Finding your own ideal cadence improves your long-distance and uphill endurance.

Pedalling Speed

The speed you pedal at makes a big difference to your cycling. Pedalling too slowly is hard work, and tires you out quickly. Pedalling too fast means you end up travelling more slowly than you need to, without putting enough pressure on the pedals. All riders pedal at a slightly different cadence, but aiming for one pedal stroke per second is a good place to start.

Shifting Technique

To keep your cadence at one pedal revolution per second, you need to be in the correct gear (see page 15). Shifting gear smoothly is a skill:

1) Make sure you can find the gear shift levers with your fingers without looking at them. Keep your eyes on where you are going!

2) Slightly ease off the pressure on the pedals. Keep them turning, but do not press down hard.

3) Quickly shift gear. Don't put full pressure on the pedals until the gear has completely changed.

Bradley Wiggins

Great Britain
Date of birth: 28 April, 1980
Height: 1.9m
Weight: 69kg

Bradley Wiggins is a professional racing cyclist who has a glittering career both on the track and the road. He began as a track cyclist, winning a gold medal at both the World Championships in 2003 and the Olympic Games in 2004. He then began to concentrate on road racing, although he still competed and won gold medals in the 2007 and 2008 track World Championships, and on the track in the Olympic Games of 2008.

2012 was a fantastic year for Wiggins. He won both the prestigious Tour de France and an Olympic gold medal in the time trial at the London Olympic Games. He is the only cyclist to date to win the Paris–Nice race, the Tour de Romandie, the Critérium du Dauphiné and the Tour de France in a single season. In 2013 Bradley Wiggins was granted a knighthood by the queen for his achievements, and became Sir Bradley Wiggins.

Shifting Gear

1 On flat ground, the rider will probably be in one of her middle gears – the chain will be on one of the middle cogs on the back wheel.

Picking the right gear for the type of slope you are riding on makes cycling quicker and easier.

2 As the rider starts to go uphill, she shifts to a lower gear, with the chain on a bigger cog on the back wheel. This lower gear is easier to pedal.

3 Coming downhill, the rider shifts to a higher gear, with the chain on a small cog on the back wheel. The bike is harder to pedal, but gravity is helping to pull it downwards!

Using Gears

Using the right gear allows you to keep pedalling at one revolution per second, whether you are going uphill, downhill or along flat ground.

- The lowest gear is the one that's easiest to pedal. If you choose a low gear on flat ground, your legs will be spinning fast just to keep going at walking speed. But for riding up steep hills, low gears are a cyclist's biggest friend.

- A high gear is much harder to pedal, and would be impossible to use going up a steep hill. For coming DOWN a steep hill, though, high gears are great!

Most riders use a middle gear most of the time. Bikes usually have shifters that allow you to change two or three gears at a time. This can be very useful if a hill turns out to be a lot steeper than you expected!

Uphill Riding Skills

One of the things many people hate when they start cycle racing is riding uphill. But a few coaching tips can make cycling uphill much easier – and some people even end up enjoying it!

Uphill Cadence

Many riders find it is a good idea to pedal in a low gear and at a slightly higher cadence (pedalling speed) than normal when going uphill. This saves energy, and means that if the slope ahead gets steeper you will be able to carry on without having to change gear again. A high cadence is especially useful when riding uphill off-road. Here, obstacles such as rocks and tree roots can easily slow the bike down or throw you off balance.

Riding Uphill

1 As the riders approach the hill, they pick what they think will be the right gear to help them get up the slope.

2 The riders sitting down have chosen a low gear and can ride with a good body position. They are sitting down, their weight is forward on the bike and their elbows bent. The bike is easy to pedal in a straight line.

3 Further up the slope, the rider standing on the pedals starts to fall back. He has used up too much energy pedalling in a higher gear, and cannot keep up.

Murphy's Mile

The first cyclist ever to ride a mile in a minute was Charles Minthorn Murphy of the USA. He managed a time of 57.8 seconds – cycling behind a train, on a special boarded-in track!

Body Position

The photo sequence on page 16 shows a good uphill riding body position for the seated riders. They are using a lower gear and a higher cadence than than the rider who is standing up.

This rider is demonstrating terrible technique! As he pulls on the handlebars, the wheels zig and zag from side to side, meaning he cycles further than if he was travelling in a straight line.

To Stand or Not to Stand?

When pushing uphill, some riders achieve bursts of extra power and speed by standing on the pedals and rocking the handlebars from side to side. It is important to make sure the bike does not start zigzagging across the road – you should always keep the wheels pointing straight uphill.

Standing up on the pedals drains a rider's energy far more quickly than sitting on the saddle and pedalling steadily. It is a technique that should only be used in short bursts, for example to catch up during a race.

● It's a Fact

Possibly the greatest uphill racer ever was the Spanish rider Federico Bahamontes. He climbed so fast that he was nicknamed the 'Eagle of Toledo'.

Downhill Riding Skills

Downhill mountain-bike races are among the most exciting bike events to take part in, and certainly the most spectacular to watch. The skills and techniques of the riders, at speeds where a crash can result in serious injury, are breathtaking.

Key Skills

The same key skills used by downhill racers can be learned and used by other cyclists. These skills fall into three main areas:

1) Body position

The key skill here is to keep your weight far back on the bike. Some riders even hang their bottom off the seat, resting their stomach on it instead. This makes it less likely that they can be thrown over the handlebars, and gives a more streamlined riding position.

British rider Matt Simmonds at the Ponte de Lima downhill international race in Portugal, 2014. Like Manon Carpenter, Simmonds rides for the Madison Saracen team.

Bent elbows make controlling the bike easier, especially if the front wheel drops down or hits an obstacle.

Eyes focused ahead, looking towards the next bend or drop-off rather than looking down at the ground immediately in front.

Bent knees keep the weight back and Sam's body upright, so that he is able to keep looking ahead. They also act as shock absorbers.

Low saddle allows Sam to keep his weight well back on the bike, balanced between the front and rear wheels.

Heels down and toes pointing slightly upwards to help control the bike using the pedals.

18

2) Cornering

The 'vanishing point' (see the photo below) can help you to judge the right speed into a corner. If the vanishing point is moving closer, slow down. If it is moving away, speed up.

3) Braking

Brake smoothly. The front brake is more powerful, but it is important to use some back brake as well to stop the rear wheel lifting up and tipping you off.

Vanishing point

Manon Carpenter

Great Britain
Date of birth: 11 March, 1993
Team: Madison Saracen

Welsh star Manon Carpenter is a professional racing cyclist who specialises in downhill mountain bike racing. She had a magical season in 2014, winning both the UCI World Cup Mountain Bike Downhill Series title in Meribel, France, and the UCI Mountain Bike World Championships, in Hafjell, Norway.
Her junior career successes include the Junior UCI Downhill World Championship and the Junior UCI Mountain Bike World Cup.
Manon was introduced to mountain bike racing by her father who is a BMX track builder, and her coach.

The point where the two edges of the road appear to meet is called the 'vanishing point'. Expert riders use the vanishing point as a way of judging their speed.

Ollies

Ollies, or jumps, are a key part of every BMX rider's set of skills, whether doing tricks or racing. They can also be useful for other kinds of cyclist.

BMX

Ollies are the basis of many BMX tricks on the street or ramp. Ollies are also a key skill for BMX racers, who steer their bikes round a dirt track that has banked curves (berms), tight curves and tabletops (steep ramps with a raised, flat area of earth between them). Being able to ollie your bike over these, instead of riding them, gives racers a big advantage.

1 Standing up on the pedals, give one of them a hard push while pulling up on the handlebars. The front wheel will rise off the ground.

2 Bring your weight forwards and roll your wrists forwards slightly. This will bring the back wheel up into the air as well. (If you're wearing pedals with clips or toeclips, these make lifting the back wheel a lot easier.)

Riding High

The world's highest aerial on a bike was performed by the legendary BMX ramp rider, Mat Hoffman. He launched his bike over 15 metres into the air, and landed safely.

Non-BMX riders

Being able to ollie is useful for mountain bikers, who often have to get over tree roots, logs, rocks and other obstacles. Even road riders benefit from knowing how to ollie, as long as they are completely expert at it. Most roads have a good selection of kerbs, drainage covers, holes and other obstacles, and being able to do a little jump to lift your wheels over these can be very useful.

Shanaze Reade

Great Britain
Date of birth: 23 September, 1988
Height: 1.7m
Weight: 79kg

Shanaze Reade became one of the world's top BMX racers when she won the Junior World Championship in 2006. She went on to be UCI BMX World Champion in 2007, 2008 and 2010. Showing that she's no one-trick pony, Shanaze is also a top track cyclist. In 2007 and 2008 she won the World Team Sprint Championship with Victoria Pendleton. (Victoria is another of Britain's top riders, and a World Individual Sprint Champion.)

3 Keeping your balance, land the bike either back wheel first or both wheels together. (It's dangerous to land on the front wheel, as you almost always get flipped over the handlebars.) Ride away wearing a big grin!

Road Racing

Road racing first became popular in the early 1900s. Today, road races take many forms, usually involving riding from place to place with a group of other riders.

Race Distances

There are several different distances of road race. Some last just a few hours. In short races such as these, the first rider across the line wins. Other races, called stage races, go on for days. In these multi-day events, the rider with the fastest overall time wins.

Time Trials

A time trial is a bike race against the clock. Time trialling in Britain started because racing bicycles on

1 Road riders use a 'chain gang' like this one to cover ground fast. The rider in front keeps up the pace, while those behind have an easier ride in his slipstream.

2 After his turn in front, the rider drops to the back of the group for a slight rest. A new rider takes over at the front. The first rider slowly makes his way back up the line as the others take a turn at the front and then drop back.

open roads was not allowed until 1942. Cyclists began to organise secret events, where they would set off one after the other along a pre-determined route. The winner was the rider who finished the route in the fastest time. This is still how time trials work today.

Sportives

Bike events called sportives are growing increasingly popular among non-competition road cyclists. Groups of riders follow a set route, sometimes over several days. Sportives are not strictly competitions, but because they're timed, people do race each other. They are open to riders of most ages and abilities.

Only the rider's head and shoulders create air resistance.

Chest and stomach are parallel to the ground.

Hands on the 'dropped' part of the handlebars.

Bent back keeps the rider's front low down.

Racers try to hold a good, fast, aerodynamic position.

Track Racing

Track racing, like road racing, has been around for over 100 years. Racers ride on purpose-built oval tracks with banked bends. The racing is spectacular, and in some track events crashes are common.

Track Bikes

Track bikes are usually fixed-wheel. This means they have only one gear, and the rider's legs keep turning all the time the back wheel is going round. Track bikes do not have brakes, and the only way to slow down is to pedal more slowly. Riding one for the first time feels a bit like being on a runaway train!

1 The racer gets into position, with the front wheel of the bike on the line. Either an assistant comes and grips the back wheel between his legs, or the bike is positioned with its back wheel in an automatic starting machine. With the bike held solid, the rider clips his shoes into the pedals.

2 The starting signal goes off and the rear wheel is released. The rider stands up on the pedals in order to get up to speed as quickly as possible.

Track Events

There are many different track events. These are the main ones:

• Sprint

Two riders start together, with the aim of crossing the line first. They do not go flat out from the start – in fact, they sometimes end up balancing motionless on their bikes, or barely moving at all! This is because it's much easier to win coming from behind, so each rider tries to go as slowly as possible until the very last moment, so that he or she can speed in from the back.

• Pursuit

In the team pursuit, two teams of four riders start on opposite sides of the track. The fastest goes through to the next round. The individual pursuit has one rider on each side.

• Time trial

This is a flat-out race, in which the fastest time wins. It is raced over 1 kilometre for men and 500 metres for women.

Laura Trott

Great Britain
Date of birth: 24 April, 1992
Height: 1.63
Weight: 52kg

Laura Trott is a professional track cyclist specialising in the team pursuit and omnium events. As well as the two gold medals she won at the 2012 Olympic Games in London, she also has an impressive 7 European Championship gold medals, 5 UCI World Championship gold medals, and a Commonwealth Games gold medal.

In 2012, Laura together with Joanna Rowsell and Dani King broke the world record twice in the team pursuit in one day.

During team time-trial events, the riders use a similar chain gang technique to the one shown on page 22.

Off-Road Racing

There are two main forms of off-road racing: cyclo-cross and mountain biking. Of these, cyclo-cross is older, and mountain biking more popular.

Cyclo-cross

Cyclo-cross first became popular as a way for road riders to keep fit during the winter, when it was tricky to train on the roads. Today it is a competitive event in its own right. Sometimes riders race round a circuit for a set period of time, often an hour. The winner is the one who goes furthest. Sometimes the race is over a set distance, with the winner being the first one over the line.

Mountain Biking

There are three main types of mountain-bike racing:

1) Cross-country, usually called XC, which is a bit like a one-day road race but off-road.

2) Downhill, a timed run down a set course, a bit like ski racing.

Cyclo-cross racers have to carry their bikes over obstacles, or up hills that are too steep and muddy to ride.

3) 4x or dual, where riders race side-by-side down a technical course.

Each of these types has specialist bikes and skills. Many racers ride both downhill and 4x, but at the top level none mix XC with either of the other two. XC racers have more in common with road riders, with the emphasis on endurance and sprinting power, rather than bike handling skills.

24-hour Racing

Twenty-four hour racing is increasingly popular with non-professional riders. These are off-road races that last a day and a night. The winner is the person or team who manages the most whole laps in 24 hours. People enter either solo or as a relay team of two or four riders. At most 24-hour races there is a party atmosphere, with as much emphasis on having fun as there is on winning.

Mechanical skills are important for all bike racers, but especially mountain bikers, whose bikes take a lot of punishment during a race.

A typical modern cross-country hardtail mountain bike (with front suspension but no rear): a steel frame, 110-mm-travel forks (which can move up to 110mm to absorb shocks), wide handlebars and 27 gears for dealing with just about any hill.

Statistics and Records

Road Racing

This table shows the riders with the most wins in the 'Grand Tours' (the Tour de France, the Giro d'Italia in Italy, and the Vuelta e España in Spain):

Name:	Total wins:	Tour:	Giro:	Vuelta:
Eddy Merckx (Belgium, b.1945)	11	5	5	1
Bernard Hinault (France, b.1954)	10	5	3	2
Jacques Anquetil (France, 1934–87)	8	5	2	1
Miguel Indurain (Spain, b.1964)	7	5	2	0
Fausto Coppi (Italy, 1919–60)	7	2	5	0
Alberto Contador (Spain, b.1982)	6	2	1	3
Gino Bartali (Italy, 1914–2000)	5	2	3	0
Alfredo Binda (Italy, 1902–86)	5	0	5	0
Felice Gimondi (Italy, b.1942)	5	1	3	1
Tony Rominger (Switzerland, b.1961)	4	0	1	3

Track Cycling

This table shows world record-holders as they stood in early 2015.

Event:	Rider and country:	Year:
Men's sprint	François Pervis, France	2013
Women's sprint	Kristina Vogel, Germany	2013
Men's individual pursuit	Jack Bobridge, Australia	2011
Women's individual pursuit	Sarah Hammer, USA	2010
Men's 1-km time trial	François Pervis, France	2013
Women's 500-m time trial	Anna Meares, Australia	2013
Men's team pursuit	Great Britain	2012
Women's 3000-m team pursuit	Great Britain	2012
Women's 4000-m team pursuit	Australia	2015

Mountain Biking

This table shows the riders with the most cross-country racing medals at world mountain bike championships as of early 2015 (in order of number of gold medals):

Men's:	Medals:	Women's:	Medals:
1 Julien Absalon, France	7	1 Gunn-Rita Dahle Flesjå, Norway	6
2 Nino Schurter, Switzerland	5	2 Alison Sydor, Canada	10
3 Henrik Djernis, Denmark	4	3 Margarita Fullana, Spain	4
4 Roland Green, Canada	3	4 Irina Kalentieva, Russia	5
5 Thomas Frischknecht, Switzerland	7	5 Paola Pezzo, Italy	4
6 Christoph Sauser, Switzerland	4	6 Julie Bresset, France	2
7 Miguel Martinez, France	3	7 Maja Wloszczowska, Poland	5
8 Filip Meirhaeghe, Belgium	4	8 Sabine Spitz, Germany	5

Glossary

Aerodynamic Describes something that is designed to reduce air resistance and so increase speed.

Air resistance The slowing-down effect of air on a moving object.

Banked Built to be steep-sided. A banked turn is built up on the outside, so that it forces the bike and rider to lean over.

Berm A banked turn.

Cycle lane A special lane set aside for cyclists to use.

Digestive To do with the digestion (breaking down inside the body) of food.

Drop-off A steep, sudden, and sometimes vertical descent on a mountain-bike trail.

Endurance The ability to do something for a long time.

Fluorescent Describes something that shines brightly when hit by light.

Keirin A track race that starts behind a pacer, often a small motor bike, and finishes with a sprint for the line.

Omnium A track event that takes place over more than one day and includes several different races.

Pollution Harmful substances such as gases released by vehicles, which cause damage to the environment.

Shifts In cycling, 'shifting' means either changing gear or moving very fast.

Slipstream A pocket of still air behind another rider, where there is less air resistance to fight against.

Spirit level A tube of liquid with an air bubble in the middle. When the air bubble is in the centre of the tube, it means the tube is perfectly level.

Stage In a stage race, cyclists ride a set route each day, calle a 'stage'.

Tabletop Steep slopes with a raised, flat area in-between.

Time trial A race against the clock.

Toeclips Devices attached to pedals that hold the rider's toes to give them extra grip.

Velodrome An arena for track cycling, with an oval track and steeply banked ends.

Websites

www.britishcycling.org.uk

The website of British Cycling, where you can get help in finding a cycling club near you. British Cycling has a programme called Go-Ride, which aims to encourage young people into cycling.

www.letour.fr/le-tour

The home site of the world's most popular bike race, the Tour de France. Here you can find out the route the Tour is taking each year, the teams and riders involved, and the history of the race.

www.uci.ch

The website of the Union Cycliste Internationale, the world governing body for cycling. The site has information about the different competition cycling events, plus results from competitions around the world.

www.bikehub.co.uk

This Bicycle Association site aims to help people use their bikes for fun, fitness and transport, and is less concerned with competition cycling.

Note to parents and teachers: every effort has been made by the Publishers to ensure that these websites are suitable for children, that they are of the highest educational value, and that they contain no inappropriate or offensive material. However, because of the nature of the Internet, it is impossible to guarantee that the contents of these sites will not be altered.
We strongly advise that Internet access is supervised by a responsible adult.

Index